SEE IT, DREAM IT, DO IT

How 25 people just like you found their dream jobs

COLLEEN NELSON & KATHIE MACISAAC

With illustrations by **SCOT RITCHIE**

pajamapress

First published in Canada and the United States in 2023

Text copyright © 2023 Colleen Nelson, Kathie MacIsaac
This edition copyright © 2023 Pajama Press Inc.
This is a first edition.
10 9 8 7 6 5 4 3 2 1

The publisher gratefully acknowledges the support of the Canada Council for the Arts and the Ontario Arts Council for its publishing program. We acknowledge the financial support of the Government of Canada through the Canada Book Fund (CBF) for our publishing activities.

Library and Archives Canada Cataloguing in Publication
Title: See it, dream it, do it : how 25 people just like you found their dream jobs / Colleen Nelson
    & Kathie MacIsaac ; with illustrations by Scot Ritchie.
Names: Nelson, Colleen, author. | MacIsaac, Kathie, author. | Ritchie, Scot, illustrator.
Description: First edition. | Includes index.
Identifiers: Canadiana 20230219780 | ISBN 9781772782882 (hardcover)
Subjects: LCSH: Success in business—Juvenile literature. | LCSH: Successful people—
    Biography—Juvenile literature. | LCSH: Vocational guidance—Juvenile literature. | LCSH:
    Occupations—Juvenile literature. | LCGFT: Biographies.
Classification: LCC HF5381.2 .N455 2023 | DDC j331.702—dc23

Publisher Cataloging-in-Publication Data (U.S.)
Names: Nelson, Colleen, author. | MacIsaac, Kathie, author. | Ritchie, Scot, illustrator.
Title: See It, Dream It, Do It : How 25 People Just Like You Found Their Dream Jobs / Colleen Nelson
    and Kathie MacIsaac ; with illustrations by Scot Ritchie.
Description: Toronto, Ontario Canada : Pajama Press, 2023. | Includes index. | Summary:
    "This nonfiction career resource features twenty-five diverse jobs and people. Using full-color
    photos, these profiles explore how each individual was able to achieve their dream job, and what
    their dream job entails. This includes their areas of study, relevant job experience and more.
    Spin-off jobs, fun facts, pro tips round out this career guide, as well as spotlight features on
    children currently working toward their dream jobs. Also included a table of contents, a glossary,
    an index, and reference"— Provided by publisher.
Identifiers: ISBN 978-1-77278-288-2 (hardcover)
Subjects: LCSH: Occupations -- Biography-- Juvenile literature. | Job descriptions - Juvenile
    literature. | Vocational guidance - Juvenile literature. | BISAC: JUVENILE NONFICTION /
    Careers. | JUVENILE NONFICTION / Biography & Autobiography / General. | JUVENILE
    NONFICTION / Diversity & Multicultural.
Classification: LCC CT107.N457 |DDC 920.02- dc23

Cover and interior illustrations—Scot Ritchie
Cover and book design—Lorena González Guillén

Printed in China by WKT Company

Pajama Press Inc.
11 Davies Avenue, Suite 103, Toronto, Ontario Canada, M4M 2A9

Distributed in Canada by UTP Distribution
5201 Dufferin Street Toronto, Ontario Canada, M3H 5T8

Distributed in the U.S. by Publishers Group West, Ingram Content Group
1 Ingram Blvd. La Vergne, TN 37086, USA

For James, who has just graduated
and is on the way to finding
his dream job

–C.N.

To Cameron, for encouraging and
supporting my dreams

–K.M.

CONTENTS

FOREWORD

When someone asks, "What do you want to be when you grow up?", you might have an answer ready. But you also might have no idea! A lot of young people feel pressure to figure out what career path they want to pursue. With so many jobs out there, how do you narrow it down? Or know which job is right for you? How do you find out what skills and education are required? In this book, we try to answer some of those questions for you by introducing twenty-five inspiring individuals who found their dream job.

As we spoke with people about how they got their jobs, what they actually do in a day, and what steps they dream of taking next, we found that, back in middle school or high school, many of them never imagined they would end up where they are today. We heard again and again that keeping an open mind and trying new things led them in unexpected directions, so we encourage you to do the same as you think about your future.

We hope you discover something in these profiles that sparks an interest in you and helps you start heading down your own path. **Keep dreaming!**

The jobs we wish existed

Colleen: professional puppy cuddler
Kathie: professional chocolate-chip cookie tester

The one that got away
We wish we could have interviewed...
Colleen: an astronaut
Kathie: a race car driver

The job we could never do
It might be right for some people, but not for us!

Colleen: Professional sports coach. I just want everyone to have fun. Also, I'd feel bad for the losing team.
Kathie: Mountain climbing guide. I think the view would be fantastic, but I don't like heights, so I'd be afraid to look at it!

ACE RODRIGUEZ

– Fitness Trainer / Coach –

> **"** I love movement. It makes my mind and my body feel good. **"**

Being a fitness trainer and coach encapsulates everything Ace wanted to be when they were growing up. Ace has always loved being active, playing sports, and teaching others, so after high school they started a four-year undergrad degree in **kinesiology**, which could have led to careers like physiotherapy or physical education. Eventually Ace realized that becoming a personal fitness trainer was more in line with what they wanted to do. From their own lived experiences, and as a member of the 2SLGBTQIA+ community, Ace knew that there were people who also had negative experiences at the gym. Ace wanted to show that fitness can be inclusive, empowering, and enjoyable for everyone. They decided to switch into a two-year fitness **diploma** program that included a practicum of 100 hours.

PRO TIP

Traditional gyms aren't the only places to work out. Try finding outdoor fitness trails or a local playground to get creative with exercise.

A practicum is a way to get hands-on experience with a trained professional.

★ WHY NOT TRY ★

A new sport. Learning different types of movement is a great way to help your body get strong and stay healthy.

Once the course work was finished and the final exam passed, Ace was hired by their supervising trainer, Geoff. Geoff had the same fitness **philosophy** as Ace: movement is for everyone and we all deserve to move our bodies in any way that brings us joy. When Ace is working with a client, there are no treadmills or jumping jacks. Ace focuses on low-impact strength training. Just like Ace, Geoff believes fitness should be **accessible** to all people regardless of size, gender, sexuality, age, ethnicity, or ability. Both Ace and Geoff strive to foster an environment that is free from pressure and judgment.

Ace works with individual clients in a private gym, so every day is different, and the start time depends on the client's schedule or the gym's availability. When working with a new client, Ace discusses goals and does a baseline assessment to see where the **areas of opportunity** lie. As a client progresses, Ace changes the program and introduces new exercises.

Being a fitness trainer involves a lot of listening and counseling. As Ace builds rapport with clients, they love to see them gain confidence in movement. As Ace says, "Fitness training and coaching is more than just lifting a bar. You have to be an empathetic person and try to make real connections with your clients."

LIVING the DREAM

SAM SCALETTA was ten when they started taking parkour classes at a local movement center. The classes challenged students to jump, leap, and flip using the apparatus in the studio. When Sam was thirteen, they became a junior coach and helped with birthday parties and lessons. A few months later, Sam moved into a coaching position and is now able to lead training sessions.

INSPIRING INDIVIDUALS

DR. WENDY SUZUKI is a fitness instructor and a professor of neural science and psychology. According to her research, exercise isn't just good for the body. It also stimulates the birth of new brain cells in the part of the brain that promotes imagination and creativity.

SPIN-OFF JOBS

★ Nutritional counselors help people improve their physical and mental health through understanding their relationship with food.

★ Physical education teachers plan and deliver phys ed curriculum to their students. They also encourage a healthy lifestyle through movement and nutrition.

★ Athletic therapists work with athletes to treat muscle, bone, and joint injuries. They are often on field during sports games in case emergency care is needed.

EVERY BODY STRONGER

ANGIE ARAGON
– Skydiving Instructor –

"You don't know that you want to be doing it all the time until you actually try it."

Angie never imagined herself as a skydiving instructor; she wanted to be a corporate-level businesswoman. An entry-level accounting position at a real estate company turned into an **internship** as a real estate agent, and Angie became well known in her profession. She had the lifestyle she'd always dreamed of, but a chance to go skydiving in New Zealand completely changed the trajectory of her life.

After her first jump, Angie knew she wanted to get her skydiving license. It took her two months and several jumps to reach that goal. She could see that the lifestyle of the skydivers she met at a drop zone was very different from her corporate lifestyle. Angie was drawn to the freedom to travel, the independence, the challenges, and the opportunity to disconnect from a demanding career. She decided to give up real estate and pursue a skydiving instructional rating.

Angie trained to take people on tandem skydives. This is where an individual is strapped to an instructor, and they jump together. She was one of the first females in this physically demanding job, and gaining respect and acceptance in the field was challenging. Five years later, she pursued an examiner rating, allowing her to train other skydiving instructors. In 2016, she was one of the only female examiners in the United States. Some people didn't want to be taught by a woman in a field that men primarily dominated, but Angie was passionate about her work and continued to push forward.

SPIN-OFF JOBS

★ **Riggers** make sure skydiving equipment is safe and functional.

★ **Jump pilots** specialize in flying aircraft for skydiving.

★ **Videographers** capture the skydiving experience in the air for clients.

Angie now runs a business with her husband called USPACourses.com. She travels to many different locations to teach people who are already experienced in skydiving to become instructors. At the end of her courses, she can supply USPA (United States Parachute Association) certification. Angie loves helping instructors obtain the knowledge and ratings they need to teach others to become skydivers.

Summer is the busy season for skydiving, and Angie has very few days off between April and September. She doesn't have a set work schedule, and she may be in a different drop zone every four to five days. As an examiner, it's crucial that Angie reads and interprets the stress levels of her students. Since she's the first passenger a tandem instructor will have, she needs to be sure she's comfortable that they can respond to an emergency or a malfunction before she jumps with them.

Since she's fluent in Spanish, Angie is in high demand in Latin America. There are very few bilingual skydiving examiners, and it's challenging to teach a course when you need a translator to pass along information. Angie feels lucky that her job allows her to travel and share her passion with others worldwide.

INSPIRING INDIVIDUALS ★

At twenty-one years of age, **ANAMIKA SHARMA** is the youngest, and one of only a handful, of women with a professional skydiving license in India. Trained by a family friend and her father since her first skydiving experience at age eleven, Anamika has made more than forty jumps and trains to compete professionally while also pursuing a university degree.

★ WHY NOT TRY ★

Riding on a rollercoaster to see if you like the feeling of plunging from a height.

PRO TIP

There is a calculated risk involved in skydiving, but listening, following instructions, and staying on top of procedures all minimize the potential for dangerous incidents.

DID YOU KNOW?

There is a team of all-female professional skydivers? Highlight Pro Skydiving Team is comprised of thirteen talented women who encourage women and girls through demonstration jumps, presentations, and sharing their stories of inspiration.

DARYL FLETCHER
— Ranch Owner / Equine Therapist —

"Don't be afraid to fail. Don't be afraid to mess up. Don't be afraid to try.**"**

Daryl's first encounter with a horse was a pony ride as a child. He found it exhilarating and freeing. He also loved the summers he spent with his grandparents on their farm and the hard work and life lessons he learned there. When Daryl became a youth pastor as an adult, he dreamed of having a place where he could mentor kids. He wanted to teach them to ride horses while building character through doing farm work and developing skills, but it took many years for his dream to become a reality.

Daryl was a barn manager in Maryland while working as a pastor. He didn't own a horse until he was gifted one in his thirties. He later inherited two more. In 2014, he became a certified life coach and public speaker. He started saving money for his dream of owning a ranch. When Daryl learned about equine therapy, he realized he had found a way to combine his passion for horses with his work coaching people.

To become an equine specialist in mental health and learning (ESMHL), there is a three-phase certification during which individuals learn to understand a horse's body language and how it relates to what its rider is feeling.

★ WHY NOT TRY ★
Working at a local barn to gain experience working with horses

LIVING the DREAM

In 2019, eighteen-year-old **KHADIJAH MELLAH** became the first hijab-wearing jockey to race in England, winning the Magnolia Cup. She wanted to encourage British teens from **underrepresented** communities to get involved in horse racing. She founded the Riding A Dream Academy, which offers a scholarship program that includes a free week-long introduction to horse racing. Check out the online documentary *Riding A Dream* to learn more about Khadijah's journey.

To become an ESMHL, Daryl took PATH International's program, which consists of three phases: an onsite phase (online courses and assessment), a portfolio phase (documentation of experience), and an exam.

Horses are very sensitive and respond to the emotions that a rider experiences. Daryl's role is to talk to the client, read the horse's behavior, and help the client understand their feelings. A client may be unaware they're experiencing a specific emotion, but a horse can sense it. For example, a horse will start to move its feet, indicating that the rider is feeling anxious. Daryl can point out these actions to clients and help them address behavioral issues or challenges. He is responsible for the well-being of the horse and its rider. He loves seeing a client have a breakthrough and understand how to change their life for the better.

Daryl now owns and operates SOOFA (Stretch Out On Faith Again) Ranch in Palmetto, Georgia. SOOFA is a non-profit organization offering equine-assisted therapy, trail rides, and lessons. Many of Daryl's clients are Black or other people of color without horse experience. He loves helping individuals build confidence, address mental health issues, and learn to communicate more effectively. He wants kids to know that there are no wins or losses, only wins and learns. Daryl wants SOOFA Ranch to be a place that surrounds people with opportunities to learn and grow.

PRO TIP

In talk therapy, a therapist uses probing questions to help a client recall from memory how they felt. In equine therapy, the therapist can see how a client feels about a memory by interpreting their horse's behavior, and they help them deal with that emotion.

SPIN-OFF JOBS

★ Farriers care for horses' hooves and the shoes they may need to wear.

★ Equine dentists specialize in diagnosing, preventing, and treating issues with a horse's mouth or teeth.

★ Jockeys ride horses in races.

DAVID FORTIN
— Architect —

> 66 I work with people to envision the future. 99

As an architect, David translates people's wishes into reality. He designs places for people to live, play, and work, and has tackled more challenging projects like building houses in remote northern communities. David, who is **Métis**, is the first Indigenous person to direct a school of architecture. Throughout his career he has worked with Indigenous communities to reclaim and celebrate Indigenous architecture. He has also renovated modern buildings to express contemporary Métis design.

David starts by meeting with his clients to determine the scope of a project. Then he and his team work on the **conceptual** design. David compares his job to that of the conductor of an orchestra. He coordinates engineers, builders, electricians, plumbers, landscape designers, and ecologists so they are all playing the same song. He must balance the creative and technical sides of a design with the realities of the location. David always asks himself, "How will this impact the community?"

Some universities offer a four-year bachelor of environmental design degree, or an architectural studies degree. To become an architect, students must follow their **bachelor's degree** with a two-year **master's degree** program and then intern for another two or three years to gain experience. The final step is to take an exam that focuses on technical and safety regulations—a very important part of designing buildings. Only architects who have passed the exam receive an architectural seal,

★ WHY NOT TRY ★
Walking around your city. Take pictures of buildings that you find interesting and beautiful.

PRO TIP
Be patient. It takes years to gain enough experience to be the lead designer on a big project.

which is a special tool used to stamp a design document, showing that an architect has reviewed and approved the design.

An environmental design degree can lead to other master's programs like landscape design and interior design. You could even use this degree to further your study in furniture design or historic building preservation.

There are many facets to being a good architect. It isn't just about design. Architects also have to be good communicators. David often collaborates with other designers, architects, and engineers. He also discusses and revises plans with construction crews, gives presentations to clients, and meets with planning and zoning officers.

David's goal is always to create something pleasing to the eye. Limits like budget and space can make that a challenge, but finding a solution is what makes architecture rewarding. As David says, "Architects aren't just designing buildings; we're building community."

SPIN-OFF JOBS

★ City planners manage and design cities with an eye to the future.

★ Architectural technologists use computer software to render an architect's designs into building plans.

INSPIRING INDIVIDUALS

Determined to create opportunities for other Black girls interested in architecture, **TIFFANY BROWN** founded 400 Forward. The program's mission is to encourage more girls from underrepresented communities to pursue careers in architecture and design. Tiffany believes that supporting and mentoring young Black women will give them the tools they need to create the cities they want to live in.

DAVID SOLANO
— Teacher / Basketball Coach —

66 I believe in the community of the classroom. **99**

Like many kids, David was obsessed with football and dreamed of playing for the Denver Broncos. He never considered that having a disability— shortened arms bent at the wrist due to a condition called arthrogryposis—might limit his chances to turn his love of sport into a career. And it didn't, although his passion led him in a direction he didn't originally predict. Today he is a teacher and basketball coach at an elementary school in the same neighborhood where he grew up.

It was thinking about the influence of the people who helped him in school that drove David's decision to become a teacher. He never had a disabled Hispanic man as a role model, and he wanted a career where he could be that for kids. He received his education degree in 1998. For more than twenty-three years since then, David has been at the front of the classroom, making kids feel welcome and appreciated while also encouraging them to excel.

But David also loved playing basketball. He decided to sign up to be a summer league volunteer basketball coach. He took the knowledge he gained watching coaches from the Denver Broncos and developed his own style. After six successful years as a volunteer, David applied for a paid coaching position in the school district. He was turned down several times. At his final interview, he guaranteed a state championship win if they hired him, and that's exactly what happened his first year as their coach.

In 2016, a knee injury left David unable to walk long distances or play sports. He started using a wheelchair which he propelled by his feet. Around this time, David

LIVING the DREAM

The influence of her female coaches from high school led **KAREN WEATHERINGTON** to pursue a career as a college volleyball coach. She currently serves as the Head Coach of the Charlotte 49ers in North Carolina. Charlotte is a Division I team, which is the highest level of women's volleyball in the US. Karen is an organized person. Her role requires overseeing a large staff, recruiting and training players, managing the team's finances, and hosting summer camps to teach the sport to young people. One of the perks of her job is traveling around the world for competitions and tournaments. Her advice to anyone interested in coaching is to watch lots of volleyball and compete in a variety of sports.

was also trying to realize another dream: his own gym. He watched the kids who didn't make his school basketball team, and he wished he could give them a place to go that motivated them to do well in school.

After three years of sourcing help to set up a non-profit basketball program, David met a reporter who ran a story about his life. It made the front page of an Arizona news-paper, and soon he received donations to cover the launch of Solano's No Limit Hoops in Phoenix, Arizona, in 2018. Now, kids aged twelve to twenty can play basketball two nights a week from February to May, at no cost.

What David loves most about coaching basketball is giving kids positive and lasting memories. He also hopes he models how to be a good dad when his daughters spend time with him at practices or the gym. David credits much of his success to his mom and her tireless advocacy to open doors to opportunities for him. She always told him to shoot for the stars and never give up. David's persistence and hopeful attitude are an inspiration to the kids whose lives he touches.

★ WHY NOT TRY ★

Volunteering to assist at a recreational sports program.

SPIN-OFF JOBS

★ **Physical education teachers** instruct kids in sports, nutrition, health, and physical development.

★ **Athletic trainers** take care of the physical health of players, including prevention of and recovery from injury.

★ **Equipment managers** are responsible for purchasing, maintaining, repairing, and transporting a team's equipment and uniforms.

DEVAPRIYA CHATTOPADHYAY

— Paleontologist —

> **"** We are really interested in knowing what's going on in terms of life and how it's changing the planet through time. **"**

Devapriya loved going to the forest with her father as a child. She was a nature enthusiast, always curious about how the Earth formed and changed. When she reached high school, she chose to pursue science. A project about fossil fuels and the formation of coal sparked her interest in **geology** and earth science.

Devapriya finished her geology undergraduate degree and focused on research in her master's. She fell in love with paleontology, the study of plants and animals that existed millions of years ago. Devapriya moved to the United States to take her PhD at the University of Michigan. She wanted to teach others about fossils and ancient life. She returned to India as a faculty member and is now an associate professor in the Earth and Climate Science Department at the Indian Institute of Science Education and Research, Pune.

There are many fields within paleontology. Devapriya was interested in studying clams, snails, and other invertebrates rather than large creatures like dinosaurs. She wanted to use statistics and mathematics to understand their history, and there was lots of data to study because there are many of these types of fossils. Since India doesn't have a research museum, Devapriya started her own fossil collection.

SPIN-OFF JOBS

★ Geologists study the Earth's surface and how its makeup changes over time.

★ Mineralogists study minerals such as gold, quartz, or diamonds.

★ Oceanographers study oceans, including the animals and plants found in them.

Fieldwork is something that Devapriya loves to do. One of her current research projects is studying fossils near the Arabian Sea. Over 20 million years ago, the Arabian and Mediterranean Seas were one large body of water. Over time, it split into two separate seas. Devapriya studies the fossils to learn how the same organisms living in one body of water changed and evolved once they were separated.

Devapriya is enthusiastic about doing outreach tours for school students to teach them about fossils. She wants to expose kids to the type of science she loves but didn't learn as a kid. When she teaches university-level students, she finds it very rewarding to share her passion with others pursuing a career in her field.

Coming up with a new idea and following it until she learns if her hunch can become a proven fact is very satisfying for Devapriya. She says being inquisitive, observant, and fascinated by nature are qualities that will help someone become part of the next generation of paleontologists

LIVING the DREAM

In 2020, **NATHAN HRUSHKIN** and his dad were hiking in Horseshoe Canyon in Alberta when he came across part of a dinosaur fossil sticking out of the ground. Experts identified it as the arm bone of a 69 million-year-old hadrosaur, a duck-billed dinosaur. Nathan and his dad visited the site several more times while a team of paleontologists uncovered more bones from the location. Nathan would love to become a paleontologist, and with this significant discovery, it looks like his career is off to a great start!

PRO TIP

A background in physics, chemistry, and math helps you solve problems using numbers (also known as quantitative thinking). This type of thinking can help you learn concepts in fields related to science. Skills in computer programming can also help you decipher patterns in databases of fossils.

FAITH FUNDAL

— Radio Host / Multimedia Journalist —

"Lead from where you are."

Faith enjoyed the fast pace of the broadcasting program at their Richmond, B.C. high school. As they say, "I'm a do-er, not a be-er." Once they graduated, it was time to think about **post-secondary** education, so Faith researched colleges that would give them practical experience in journalism. The British Columbia Institute of Technology seemed like a great fit. To apply, Faith put together a portfolio (a collection of materials that showed off their skills related to communications), took a current-events and spelling test, and did an interview. Unfortunately, it was a competitive program, and Faith wasn't accepted.

Faith waited a year and applied again. During that time they worked for a newspaper and gained more experience in the media industry. Their second application was a success! BCIT's two-year program had some in-class learning about the basics of journalism, but, just like Faith hoped, most of it was hands-on—perfect for a person working with adult ADHD.

Faith's career has taken them from Vancouver to Prince George, British Columbia, and on to Winnipeg, Manitoba, where they are now the host of a radio program. Every work day, Faith and their team meet in the morning for a story

★ WHY NOT TRY ★

Listening to a podcast. From true crime to fashion to sports, there's something for everyone!

LIVING the DREAM

At fifteen years old, **TAI POOLE** was already a seasoned podcaster for his Webby-award winning podcast, *Tai Asks Why*. In each episode, Tai seeks to answer the universe's great mysteries, like "why do we dance?" and "what is infinity?" In his career, he's interviewed everyone from NASA scientists to stand-up comedians to get answers.

INSPIRING INDIVIDUALS ★

YouTuber, freelance journalist, and reporter **LUCY EDWARDS** won the chance to live her dream when she was chosen by BBC's Radio 1 to host the morning radio show. What made her success extra exciting was that she was the first blind person to do so, and her guide dog, Olga, spent the show at her feet. In addition to her YouTube channel, Lucy has worked on BBC's *Ouch* podcast and other radio programs, and has also hosted events and become the first blind Pantene UK ambassador. Lucy's engaging personality also comes across on TikTok, where 1.8 million users follow her as @lucyedwards.

SPIN-OFF JOBS

★ TV and radio producers work behind the scenes to pull shows together by finding guests, managing talent, and organizing the show's format.

★ Broadcast engineers install new systems, handle technical issues, and trouble-shoot if problems arise.

★ Reporters write and relay news stories to the public.

meeting to discuss what's going on locally, nationally, and internationally. Working with a diverse group of people is important. Everyone brings their own viewpoint to the meetings and listens to each other's ideas.

Putting together a radio program is more than just saying the lines. Along with other producers and associate producers, Faith does research, writes background and interview questions, and develops a script for each story. What Faith loves most about their job is being able to have a real conversation with someone. It's not their job to pass judgment, but to dig deep and discover what motivates their guests. "It makes my heart happy that someone feels safe enough to share their story with me."

Over Faith's career, they've worked in all aspects of media, from television to newspaper, but radio is what Faith fell in love with. Hosting their own show wasn't something that Faith had even considered—believe it or not, Faith gets stage fright!—but after hosting a podcast called *Them & Us*, they realized how much they liked the intimacy of it. With radio, there's no lights or cameras to worry about; it's just you and the audience.

Faith is always conscious of their **bias**. They know it's impossible not to have one, but being aware of what it is and how it might affect an interview ensures that Faith gives a fair report.

HAZEL BARTON

— Cave microbiologist —

" Go explore outdoors. **"**

Hazel's first experience exploring caves happened at fourteen when she attended an Outward Bound course in England. Caving soon became her hobby. Later, while a postdoctoral researcher in microbiology in the United States, Hazel worked with a renowned microbiologist who was also interested in caving. He convinced her to combine her interests and focus on cave microbiology, or the study of small microbes (like bacteria) living in caves. This was a relatively uncommon field of study in the U.S., so Hazel would be doing ground-breaking research.

Once she finished her education in 2003, Hazel became a university professor and continued doing research. She is currently a professor of biology and geoscience at the University of Akron. She teaches classes and mentors students in developing their own research about caves. Her students have studied topics like the deep, ancient lakes in Wind Cave in South Dakota, the use of carbon dioxide to make paint **opaque**, and how cave birds called swiftlets cause ropes left in caves to break down. Hazel says there still aren't many people who study caves, so the opportunities for exciting and novel research are endless.

Spending time in the field is Hazel's favorite part of her job, but it can be physically demanding. If a location is remote, she might have to go on an extensive hike to access it. She may be required to camp underground for several days,

★ WHY NOT TRY ★

Spelunking! Many places offer tours for people of all ages to explore caves. Contact an organization like the National Caves Association to find a location close to you and start planning your next family adventure.

PRO TIP

Be curious about the natural world. Grab a headlight to explore in the dark, take random turns while hiking a familiar path, and become comfortable outdoors.

carrying all her equipment and gear with her. Bugs, snakes, and spiders are common, and there may be small or tight spaces to get through. Fortunately, Hazel loves adventure and is always curious about where a cave leads.

One of Hazel's career highlights was being part of the team that discovered Cloud Ladder Hall, part of the Er Wang Dong cave system in China. This is one of the largest cave rooms in the world and, thanks to its 1,200-foot-high ceiling, it has its own weather and cloud system. Hazel also has a small start-up company that hopes to reduce the carbon footprint of making paint. The company's carbon sequestration technology uses microbes found in caves to transform carbon dioxide from the atmosphere into a product that's usable for making paint.

With so many opportunities in cave research, Hazel will never run out of topics to study. One of her dreams is to understand saltpeter, a mineral that occurs naturally in some caves and has historically been used to make explosives like gunpowder. Although caves can be dangerous, Hazel says the more knowledge you have, the safer you will be. She plans to continue climbing, crawling, and delving into the mysteries of caves for many years to come.

FUN FACT

Caves are formed in several ways. Here are a few examples:

★ **Lava tubes** are caves formed by lava after a volcanic eruption.

★ **Glacier caves** are caused by melting ice.

★ **Sea caves** occur when waves gradually erode rock along a coastline.

★ **Solution caves** (the most common type) happen when water slowly dissolves rock.

SPIN-OFF JOBS

★ **Speleologists** are scientists that specialize in the study of caves.

★ **Biotechnologists** use living organisms (like microbes) to create new technology.

★ **Cave tour operators** lead guided tours into caves and educate guests about them.

JEAN NAULT
—Forensic Artist—

> 66 Why wouldn't I do this job? It's very rewarding. 99

Jean didn't expect to use his artistic skills as an **RCMP** officer. He was five years into his policing career when he learned about composite sketches. These are drawings by a **forensic** artist who meets with victims or witnesses of a crime and draws the person they describe. Investigators circulate the image to help identify the person. Today, as part of the Missing Persons Unit in Edmonton, Alberta, Jean is one of only a handful of officers in the RCMP who do this important work.

Jean had attended the University of Alberta and received a degree in fine arts before being accepted into RCMP cadet training in 1997. Though the requirements change over time, cadet training is currently a 26-week program at Depot, the RCMP Academy in Regina, Saskatchewan.

Jean spent his first five years working as a constable in Fort McMurray, Alberta. In August 2005, he attended the FBI Academy in Virginia for a three-week course on forensic art and started doing composite sketches as soon as he returned. Later he trained to do facial reconstruction. Working with a forensic anthropologist who provides important information to Jean about the gender, approximate age,

---

★ WHY NOT TRY ★

Taking an art or drawing class offered in your community

LIVING the DREAM

BRYTON ALLARD became one of the youngest police chiefs in the United States at age twenty-one. Powers Lake Police Department hired Bryton at age nineteen, and when his supervisor decided to relocate, Bryton was recommended for the position of chief. He has been in that position since January 2022 and enjoys being actively involved in his community and connecting with residents of all ages.

and ancestry of the unknown person, he uses graphite or clay to depict what the person's face might have looked like with only their skull for reference. He also creates age-progression drawings to predict what a person who disappeared in the past might look like today.

A forensic sketch artist requires a lot of empathy, patience, and active listening skills. It can be extremely difficult for victims to watch a suspect come to life on the page, but Jean says it can also be empowering for them to know they're helping solve the crime. The time it takes to do a sketch varies, but it averages a few hours. Jean says it's important to remember that a drawing is not his; he's merely holding the pencil for the person giving the description.

Although he works a Monday-to-Friday schedule, Jean may receive a call to assist with a case at any time. There may be lulls where he doesn't sketch for a few weeks, but at other times, he may do several in one week. He stays busy with investigative work when his forensic art skills aren't needed.

Jean says he was lucky to have a good foundation in drawing and the arts, so he could later use his skills in a job he loves. He finds his work satisfying, and every day brings new challenges. He loves helping officers and the public, and he plans to continue with forensic art for the rest of his career.

PRO TIP

There are several requirements for applying to become an RCMP officer. You can learn more about the process at: https://www.rcmp-grc.gc.ca/en/how-to-apply

SPIN-OFF JOBS

★ **Pathologists** are doctors who study human bodies and tissues to determine the cause of illness or death.

★ **Detectives** help solve crimes by searching for clues and studying evidence.

★ **Art therapists** encourage people who are having difficulties or recovering from illness to use art to express and explore their feelings.

JEANNETTE MENZIES
— Ambassador of Canada to Iceland —

66 To know where you're from, to know the nation you identify with, helps you understand the world. 99

When Jeannette completed her degree in Canadian Studies, she knew her dream job would be one that let her learn and share about her home country of Canada. Since she also loved to travel and meet people, a position in the **foreign service** was a great fit.

To join the foreign service, Jeannette had to take an exam that tested her ability to deal with different scenarios. She needed to prove that she had sound judgment, since she would be representing Canada around the world. As a member of the foreign service, Jeannette has worked in many places—from Oslo, Norway, to Ankara, Turkey, to Reykjavik, Iceland, where she is currently the Ambassador of Canada. As ambassador, she represents Canada and its citizens' interests in Iceland.

Not every ambassador is a member of the foreign service. Some people get their experience in politics, the military, or business. This field of work is called **diplomacy**.

The process to become an ambassador starts a year in advance when the upcoming positions are posted. Jeannette narrowed her choices down to her top four countries and began researching each place. To explain why she would be the perfect person for the job, she focused on the skills she'd bring, not just her knowledge. Her experience in negotiation, emergency management, and Arctic issues made her the successful candidate for Iceland.

The length of an ambassador's term depends on the country. In more challenging countries, the term is one year, but in many European countries, an ambassador can expect to stay for four years.

As ambassador, Jeannette lives in the official residence of Canada in Iceland where she raises the Canadian flag every morning. She often gives speeches and has meetings with government officials, other ambassadors, and business leaders to discuss issues important to both countries. Sometimes she supports Canadian citizens in Iceland who need help, and she often speaks at trade-related events, universities, and schools. There are many evening events too, and Jeannette is often asked to give speeches in English, and sometimes in French. Jeannette is learning Icelandic and tries to incorporate it into her speeches as well.

Jeannette says the best part of her job is that it keeps changing. No two days are the same, and each day gives her a chance to learn more about her new home and to teach others about Canada.

★ WHY NOT TRY ★

Looking for opportunities to travel and study in other countries. Jeannette took an internship at the High Commission in Australia, worked as an environmental educator in Alaska, and led cycling tours through France.

SPIN-OFF JOBS

★ Mediators work with people to help them reach agreements.

★ Park interpreters protect and share information about parks.

★ Delegates for the United Nations represent their country in global meetings. They vote on important matters affecting the world.

INSPIRING INDIVIDUALS

NATHAN BALK KING attended his first model United Nations meeting as a high school student. Realizing that he was the only Native American delegate there inspired Nathan to create Model United Nations: Indigenous to encourage more students to participate. At the following year's Model United Nations, Nathan recruited twelve delegates from tribes across the United States. Through programs like Model United Nations, young people learn the value of public policy and human rights advocacy and try to find solutions for global issues.

PRO TIP

Join a speech and debate club or enter the *Concours d'art oratoire*, a French public speaking contest.

JOHN SPRAY
– Private Investigator –

66 Private investigators exist by their wits. 99

John says the library card he got when he was ten years old planted the seed for his career as a private investigator. He loved reading detective novels. As an adult, he turned his dream job into a real job when he saw an ad in the newspaper: *Wanted: Private Investigator. No experience necessary.* John spent two years learning from the more experienced private investigator and then decided to open his own agency. In the beginning, he had to do everything from answering the phone to solving cases. As Mantis Investigation got busier, John hired more investigators. Over the decades, their work has taken them all over the world from Hawaii to Germany to Jamaica.

★ WHY NOT TRY ★

Reading detective novels. See if you can figure out the culprit before the fictional detective does.

John learned how to be a private investigator on the job. Today, there are programs at community colleges that teach students the rules and regulations they need to know to pass the private investigator licensing exam.

LIVING the DREAM

After realizing someone had slashed their school's tennis court nets, a group of primary students at Brookstead State School used their investigative skills to photograph some footprints. When the vandal was nabbed for another crime, the police were able to use the photographs to get a confession.

Private investigators are hired to solve mysteries that range from **fraud** to missing persons. They use research and observation skills to find clues and crack cases. John says that learning how to talk to people is the most important part of the job.

Asking the right questions and building trust have helped John and his employees at Mantis Investigation crack over 30,000 cases.

John writes detailed reports about each case. Sometimes these reports are used as evidence in court, so it's important that the information is accurate. He has perfected **surveillance** techniques like taking good photographs and videos or staying unnoticed while following someone on foot or in a car. Some cases take a long time to solve. Patience and the ability to look at a situation from different angles are both helpful.

Police detectives also solve cases. Unlike private investigators, police officers have the power of the law on their side and can order people to talk to them. PIs don't have any legal authority and must work within the laws that govern their country.

John says the best part of his job is the adrenaline rush that comes with cracking a tough case. Whether it's talking to witnesses, tracking down embezzlers, or locating a missing person, John learns something new every time.

INSPIRING INDIVIDUALS

JAMIE KATZ is a licensed private detective in Florida who specializes in locating lost and stolen pets. Her special assistants are two trained tracking dogs, Fletcher and Gable. The dogs use a "scent article," something belonging to the missing pet, to begin the investigation. Jamie brings the dogs to the place where the pet went missing. Using their sense of smell, the dogs pick up the trail to find the pet and reunite it with its owner.

SPIN-OFF JOBS

★ Actors portray characters on stage or in films, just as private investigators often assume roles while working on a case.

★ Salespeople need to be good communicators to explain the features of their products.

★ Journalists investigate leads and share information with the public.

LEIGH GARDNER

– Park Ranger –

66 We want people to come out and see the park as a resource to utilize. **99**

Leigh grew up loving the outdoors. She was a Girl Scout throughout high school and participated in camping, hiking, and canoeing activities. After completing a science degree focused on biology, Leigh looked for seasonal opportunities with Tennessee State Parks. She spent a year working with the Junior Ranger team before applying to become a park ranger. Her university degree and work experience gave Leigh an excellent foundation to achieve her dream job.

Park rangers need a lot of training. They are police officers, so Leigh attended the Tennessee Law Enforcement Training Academy. She also took emergency medical responder (EMR) training to help people when they are hurt, and interpreter training to learn to guide people on tours. Optional training for park rangers covers other topics such as fire certification, chainsaw mastery, and rope rescue for caves and cliffs. Leigh must renew her certifications regularly; some require yearly recertification (such as gun safety), while others may be every few years (such as EMR training).

Most of Leigh's work takes place outdoors, but there's a lot of variety in her tasks. One day she might be hiking in tools and materials to build a bridge, while another day she might rescue someone lost in the woods. In addition to shift work, Leigh is sometimes **on call**, which means she must remain in the area and be available to respond to a situation quickly. Weekends are busy because more visitors means more need for park rangers, and she often works those days with a partner.

SPIN-OFF JOBS

★ Conservation officers protect wildlife, the environment, and the people interacting with them.

★ Water resource specialists are concerned with a local water supply and its quality.

★ Outdoor adventure guides organize and lead tours for guests to experience nature.

Many park rangers do a lot of student outreach. Leigh loves teaching kids about the park and encourages schools to use rangers as a local resource. She thinks kids ask some of the best questions because they are curious about why things happen. Some students attend the park for field trips, while at other times Leigh visits schools to do presentations on topics such as biology and history. She teaches people that a park is a place everyone can use and should respect. This includes throwing trash in the garbage, not approaching wildlife or taking anything out of the park, and ensuring that no fire is left unattended. Although Leigh has administrative responsibilities like event planning and grant writing, she's glad she gets to spend most of her time outdoors. Leigh says that once you have a career in the woods, leaving is hard, and she sees herself remaining a park ranger for a long time.

★ **WHY NOT TRY** ★

Approaching your local environmental office to see if they have a science project with which you can assist, such as planting milkweed for monarchs, building birdhouses for bluebirds, or counting salamanders.

PRO TIP

Flexibility, a willingness to work outside in all conditions, creativity, and strong people skills are all qualities that make a good park ranger.

LIVING the DREAM

JUDITH KASIAMA is an outdoor enthusiast who immigrated to Canada from the Democratic Republic of the Congo over a decade ago. She noticed a lack of diverse representation in the people participating in the outdoor activities she enjoyed, such as hiking, skiing, and trail running. In 2017, she founded Colour the Trails, a collective of individuals committed to showcasing and promoting diversity in the outdoors. This group organizes events, offers mentorship programs, and inspires people from all walks of life to enjoy nature. Judith hopes to motivate young people by increasing the visibility of diversity in outdoor activities. You can learn more about Colour the Trails at colourthetrails.com.

LENNA CHARLIE
– Heavy Equipment Technician –

> 66 I get to build an engine from the ground up and run equipment three times my size. 99

Lenna remembers getting called to fix the Pelly Barge's engine. It was the first day of the hunting season in a remote area of the Yukon, and people relied on the ferry. It was a lot of pressure, but Lenna worked a nineteen-hour day and managed to identify and repair the problem. Lenna, a member of the Champagne and Aishihik First Nation, has lots of stories like this one. As a heavy equipment technician, she's often in the field repairing or maintaining machinery. Working alone, and without access to a shop or parts, she has to be resourceful to get the machine running again.

Heavy equipment technicians are trained to maintain, repair, and overhaul heavy vehicles, transport trailers, heavy-duty off-road vehicles, and industrial equipment.

SPIN-OFF JOBS

★ High performance auto mechanics work on specific types of high-performance engines, like the cars driven in NASCAR races.

★ Heavy equipment operators are trained to operate four main types of equipment: backhoes, bulldozers, front-end loaders, and graders.

Lenna began her career by taking a **pre-apprentice course** at a local college. At the end of the five-month course, she wrote an exam to become an **apprentice**. Over the next four years, she rotated between taking courses for eight weeks at the Southern Alberta Institute of Technology and returning to the Yukon to complete her apprenticeship hours. Lenna received three "tickets", credentials that proved she was qualified to work in a skilled trade. Upon completion of the classroom training, the on-the-job hours, and the final exam,

Lenna received two Red Seals certifying her as a heavy equipment technician and a truck and trailer technician.

A Red Seal is an inter-provincial qualification that allows tradespeople to practice throughout Canada. In the United States, each state has its own certification program.

Female heavy equipment technicians are rare, and Lenna speaks openly about the gender-based bias she has encountered. Instead of backing down, Lenna was motivated by these experiences to show her competence and prove her naysayers wrong.

A heavy equipment technician's workday varies. Some days they are in the shop working on equipment and other days they get called to do a repair in a remote location like a mining camp, since breakdowns can happen anywhere and at any time. A lot of problem solving is required for this job because if a technician doesn't have the part needed, they have to figure out another way to get the machine running. Working as a heavy equipment technician is physically demanding work that requires attention to detail. People who work with large pieces of machinery have to be aware of their surroundings to ensure they don't get injured.

Lenna now works as an industrial training **consultant**. Her new job means she gets to go into schools to promote work in trades and oversee apprentices as they complete their hours and move on in their career. Lenna wants to inspire other young people to tackle a trade the way she did.

PRO TIP

While the need for other careers can vary, the skilled trades are always in demand. Lenna was paid to travel all over Yukon Territory as part of her job.

★ WHY NOT TRY ★

Asking to **job shadow** someone at an auto repair shop. Learning how engines work is the foundation of the trade. It was Lenna's curiosity about how heavy-duty machines ran that led her to become a technician.

FUN FACT

Did you know there is an Olympics-style competition for tradespeople? It's called WorldSkills Competition and includes sixty-two skill areas, including heavy equipment repair, floral design, brick laying, automotive auto body painting, and cyber security. Young trades-people from around the globe compete every two years for the title of international champion.

MAYSOON ZAYID
—Stand-Up Comedian / Actress—

" My job is not easy, but it is fun. "

When Maysoon was five years old, her parents put her in tap lessons. Dance was a more affordable option than physiotherapy for Maysoon's cerebral palsy. Besides gaining some great moves, Maysoon learned to be a confident performer who knows how to work a crowd.

Since childhood, Maysoon's dream was to be on the daytime soap opera *General Hospital*. It took many years, but her dream came true when she was cast as lawyer Zahra Amir.

Maysoon studied theater at university. She wanted to be an actress, but, as Maysoon says, "Hollywood doesn't cast a lot of Disabled people." She decided to pursue comedy instead. "I was lucky I was funny, or my plan would have failed miserably."

Maysoon graduated from theater school and completed a stand-up comedy class, but no class or training taught Maysoon as much as doing stand-up comedy live. When a joke falls flat, she reminds herself to never give up. After all, what other job pays you to make people laugh?

Comedians can entertain an audience by telling jokes, or by sharing funny stories. To prepare, Maysoon writes new material and practices routines to perfect her timing and flow. Like other comedians, she is also always ready to incorporate spontaneous moments with the audience into her routine.

To gain experience, comedians start out performing for five minutes or so as "openers". This is a stand-up comedian's chance to test out their best material and learn what gets a positive reaction from the crowd. A headliner is the person the audience has paid to see. Their routine lasts much longer.

> A comedian starting out has to book their own shows, or gigs. They need to call comedy club owners, send out promotional materials, and create an online presence.

PRO TIP

Maysoon recommends doing a stand-up show for family and friends, watching stand-up comedy online, or taking a stand-up comedy class.

As a comedian, Maysoon travels a lot, doing up to 200 shows a year all around the world. She is also the co-founder/co-executive producer of the New York Arab American Comedy Festival.

When Maysoon isn't on tour, she starts her day with ninety minutes of yoga to help her cerebral palsy. Then she works with her assistant from nine o'clock to three o'clock, dictating everything from movie scripts to comic books to talks on serious topics. Maysoon is an advocate for Disability rights. Her Ted Talk "I got 99 problems...palsy is just one" has been watched over six million times. She also started a charity called Maysoon's Kids to help Palestinian refugee children.

Successful stand-up comedians find humor in unexpected places. They can share it through a standard joke formula, through improv, or by telling stories. The key is to connect with an audience, which is what Maysoon does so well and has made her an inspiring individual on and off the stand-up stage.

SPIN-OFF JOBS

★ Sketch comedy writers work with a team to put together short skits.

★ On-air personalities host or emcee televised and live events, like game shows.

LIVING the DREAM

MICHAEL MCCREARY performed comedy for the first time in front of 200 people when he was only fourteen years old. He first embraced comedy as a way to support his mental health as a neurodiverse person through the program Stand Up for Mental Health, which is run by comedian and counselor David Granirer. Michael has gone on to write a memoir, *Funny, You Don't Look Autistic: A Comedian's Guide to Life on the Spectrum*, perform at comedy festivals, and consult on TV shows to ensure the authenticity of characters on the autism spectrum.

MELISSA HANEY
– Pilot –

❝I still can't believe it sometimes: I get to fly for a living!❞

Melissa wanted to travel and work with people, so she became a flight attendant with Air Inuit. She didn't expect that seeing what happened in the flight deck and learning more about the profession would make her fall in love with the idea of becoming a pilot. To be paid to fly an airplane, Melissa would have to go back to school and follow the steps to get a commercial pilot's license.

First, Melissa attended flight school at Cornwall Aviation to get her private pilot license. This allowed her to fly a plane alone within a certain distance of an airport during daylight hours with excellent visibility. The ground portion of the training included forty to eighty hours of flight exercises and maneuvers. Once Melissa had her private license, she pursued a **night rating** to fly in the dark. A multi-engine rating (for flying planes with more than one engine) came next, followed by an instrument rating (for flying in clouds or bad weather where you don't have a visual reference). Finally, commercial license training tied all the different components together.

Many factors determine how quickly an individual can get the flight hours required for their license, including access to planes, instructor availability, and weather. It took Melissa nine months. She returned to Air Inuit after her training and is now a captain. Working with a first officer and two flight attendants, she flies throughout the region of Nunavik in northern Quebec. Flights are essential here because some communities have no road access, and air travel is the only way to reach them.

SPIN-OFF JOBS

★ Aircraft maintenance technicians are responsible for installing and maintaining equipment on aircraft.

★ Air traffic controllers monitor aircraft in the skies and direct their movement.

★ Flight attendants ensure the comfort and safety of passengers on an aircraft.

Melissa can take up to eleven days off within her twenty-eight-day flight schedule. On the other days, she is either assigned to a scheduled flight or she remains on call in case she's needed to fill in for someone. Her shifts are twelve hours long, and then she must be off for twelve hours before she can fly again.

Melissa loves many aspects of her job, including the fantastic views she sees from the air and the chance to work with people who also love aviation. As a pilot, she must manage stress, stay calm in challenging situations, solve problems, and continue to build her skills throughout her career.

There are many different careers in the field of aviation. Melissa says it's important to ask questions and find a mentor to help guide you. She hopes to become a leader in her company and play a role in encouraging more women and Indigenous people to join the aviation world.

INSPIRING INDIVIDUALS

ISABEL FREDETTE always wanted to be a pilot, and an evening flight with her dad at fourteen prompted her to make her dream a reality. She had the requirements for her private pilot's license at sixteen, but she needed to wait until she turned seventeen to hold the license. Isabel continued to accrue flight hours and training until she received her commercial license at eighteen. In 2022, she became the youngest commercial pilot at True North Airways, a float plane operator and charter company. Isabel attends university during the school year and hopes to use her flight skills to assist others in the future. The sky is no limit for this young pilot!

★ WHY NOT TRY ★

Arranging a tour of an air traffic control tower or an aviation company like Nav Canada.

NEHA ARORA
— Travel Company Owner —

> 66 People told us, 'I want to do this,' and our only attitude was, 'Why not?' 99

Neha didn't go on vacations with her family as a kid. Her father is blind, her mother is a wheelchair user, and traveling was complicated because many places weren't accessible for people with disabilities. After a series of travel experiences with her family as an adult, Neha looked for solutions to their obstacles. She decided to start her own travel company so people with disabilities could travel freely and with dignity.

Neha had a degree in engineering, and she had worked in the information technology and telecom industry for several years before she started to research the travel industry. She learned about travel accessibility challenges affecting people with different types of disabilities. She spoke to management at airports and hotels to learn about the needs of their clients with disabilities. She thinks she was probably one of the least-traveled people to ever own a travel company when she started Planet Abled in 2016.

Neha juggles many roles for her business. She travels to locations to understand accessibility problems and convince people they

INSPIRING INDIVIDUALS

A trip to the Bahamas at age fifteen sparked **CORY LEE**'s passion for travel. In 2013 he started his blog, *Curb Free with Cory Lee* to share his travel adventures as a wheelchair user with spinal muscular dystrophy. Cory is now an international speaker and award-winning travel blogger with expertise in accessibility travel. He has visited all seven continents, and his bucket list includes such activities as eating sushi in Japan, cruising the Panama Canal, and visiting all fifty states in the U.S.

are important issues. She speaks at conferences to raise awareness. She trains and sensitizes drivers, hotel staff, and other service providers to meet the needs of their clients with disabilities and to treat them with respect. She also oversees her sales team and the daily operations of the company.

One of Neha's big challenges is convincing people with disabilities that they can travel. She designs tours to destinations in response to her clients' requests for certain options, such as skiing and white-water rafting. She scouts activities like horseback riding to learn how to make those experiences inclusive. She spends a great deal of time traveling, researching, and ensuring that her trips will help empower people with disabilities to travel.

Planet Abled is one of the only travel companies to offer trips that include people with and without disabilities. Neha believes we all have so much to learn from each other. A non-disabled person who sees the challenges of a person with a disability takes that knowledge home and may work to make their offices and software more accessible. A blind person understanding the challenges that a deaf person faces helps increase cross-disability awareness. Neha believes travel is a fantastic opportunity for people to grow together.

The next steps for Neha are expanding her company and creating an online platform to help match travelers to places and experiences. She is also helping to design and adapt global accessibility standards and procedures for the travel industry. Neha's dream is for everyone to have the choice and opportunity to travel and explore the world.

PRO TIP

Find a problem that's important to you or someone you care about and try to solve it.

★ WHY NOT TRY ★

Running a lemonade stand or selling items at a local market to gain business experience.

SPIN-OFF JOBS

★ **Travel agents** help people plan trips and arrange details such as accommodations, transportation, and recreation.

★ **Hotel concierges** attend to the needs of guests and provide recommendations for local services.

★ **Digital accessibility experts** help websites and mobile applications become accessible for people with disabilities.

OSCAR A. DONOSO

— Psychologist —

" I am always learning. "

Looking back, it seems obvious to Oscar that he was meant to be a psychologist. When he was younger, friends often came to him to talk about relationships. He was a good listener and became a peer counselor in high school. Then, in college, he was a residence advisor and helped students with their problems. All of these experiences made Oscar realize a career helping people was the right fit for him.

Oscar majored in psychology for his undergrad degree and then went to grad school. Another five years obtaining his **doctorate** and two years of a post-doctoral fellowship allowed Oscar to gain even more experience.

Psychologists can work in many places, including:
- hospitals
- clinics
- schools

PRO TIP

Psychology is about relationship. Oscar found ways to connect with others by being a residential advisor at his dorm, joining a multicultural club, and working as a guide to first-year college students. These roles gave him the opportunity to help and meet a wide range of people.

Some psychologists choose to go into private practice, which means they are running their own business. They are responsible for booking patients and organizing their staff. Oscar chose to work at the Children's Hospital Los Angeles, where he could specialize in working with children who have autism or who have experienced trauma. Because his patients are young, from birth to five years old, many can't talk yet, which makes parent involvement essential. Oscar, whose family is from Peru, grew up speaking Spanish.

Knowing two languages allows him to reach a wider group of people.

One of the things Oscar loves about his job is that he leads a team of professionals from many disciplines. Speech and language pathologists, **occupational therapists**, dieticians, and pediatricians discuss what they see and collaborate to come up with a treatment plan, which is explained to parents.

> Oscar uses play to observe and learn about his young patients. He can see how they cope with difficulties and teach them to redirect inappropriate behaviors. Other forms of therapy psychologists might use are art, music, and drama.

Infant mental health is a field very few people know about. One of Oscar's missions is to expand knowledge by building relationships with other professionals. He often gives presentations to trauma responders, grad students, and other psychologists and doctors. As a leader in his profession, he has trained more than 600 people.

Psychologists need perseverance, good listening skills, and strong critical thinking. A love for learning and a genuine desire to improve the lives of others are what drive Oscar to keep doing what he does.

INSPIRING INDIVIDUALS

CHRISTIAN BUCK did something important to support kids who are feeling lonely. He is credited with bringing the first Buddy Bench to North America after seeing something similar at a schoolyard in Germany. Upon his return to Roundtown Elementary School, he spoke with his principal about installing one. A Buddy Bench is a place for kids to sit when they need someone to talk to or play with. The idea caught on. Christian got national attention, and Buddy Benches have been installed all over the world thanks to his efforts.

SPIN-OFF JOBS

★ School psychologists often have a master's degree and focus on assessing and planning for children with additional needs. They work with parents, teachers and support staff.

★ Social workers help individuals, families, and communities improve their quality of life through counseling, advocacy, and reporting.

QUINLYN HADDON
— Charter Captain —

❝ My job is thrilling, rewarding, and empowering. ❞

Growing up in Ontario, Canada, Quinlyn never thought she'd be the captain of her own deep-sea fishing boat. She was fearful of the ocean as a child and never went deeper than her ankles. Things changed when she went on vacation and tried fishing on a kayak. When a fish grabbed her line and pulled her out to sea, Quinlyn's fear was replaced with excitement.

She was hooked! Quinlyn went home, but the allure of fishing called to her. She wanted to see what working on a boat would be like, so she moved to Florida and introduced herself to local charter companies, hoping that one of them would be willing to give her a chance. Her gamble paid off. She got hired to work from 4 A.M. to 10 P.M. on a sport fishing boat. At first she just watched, learning how to catch live bait, set up the rods, and drop anchor. The physicality of the job was demanding, but Quinlyn loved it and knew this was the job she wanted.

Quinlyn worked for a few years on other people's boats, moving from Florida to Mexico and Louisiana. In each location, she learned something new and gained experience catching different fish like marlin, yellowfin tuna, and swordfish. As a woman, she faced **discrimination** because a lot of captains didn't want to take a chance on her. These experiences solidified Quinlyn's intention to get her captain's license and prove them wrong.

A captain's license requires course work and sea time hours. Quinlyn received a 100-ton Master Captain's Boat License, which means she can take up to six people on her boat. Just like

SPIN-OFF JOBS

★ Marine biologists study the animals and plants in aquatic ecosystems.

★ Nature guides share their knowledge about an environment by leading expeditions by foot, kayak, boat, or bike.

when she started, Quinlyn's day begins early in the morning. First, she must catch live bait, then she heads back to the dock to prepare the fishing gear and pick up her customers. Depending on the fish, Quinlyn may stay in shallow water or she might go offshore to where the water depth is 600-2,000 feet. She enjoys teaching people how to bait and cast their lines, and to hook and reel in fish. She especially likes teaching young girls who might be unfamiliar with what fishing entails. The day ends when her boat is cleaned and docked at the marina.

Quinlyn is never complacent and is always willing to try new things. Traveling to different places has taught her new techniques and improved her skills. Fishing can be difficult. Sun, heat, and rough waters make the job physically demanding. Boat captains need to be resourceful and learn about fixing outboard motors and giving first aid, because anything can happen out on the water. Quinlyn's reward for all this is being in nature, where she never knows what she's going to see.

INSPIRING INDIVIDUALS

Fisherman and business owner **MACKIE GREEN** started the Campobello Whale Rescue Team on Campobello Island, New Brunswick. The volunteer organization rescues whales trapped in fishing gear up and down the eastern seaboard. When a tangled whale is spotted, Mackie and his team, which includes scientific advisor Dr. Moira Brown, jump in their Zodiac to help. Whales can be forty to seventy feet long or more, and cutting them free is a dangerous task. To support the volunteer operation, Mackie also runs a whale-watching business that allows him to share his respect for the ocean with others.

DID YOU KNOW?

There are three kinds of fishing:

★ Commercial fishing is for profit. The fish caught are sold.

★ Sport, or recreational, fishing is for sport, pleasure, exercise, or competition. The person who catches the fish can't sell it.

★ Subsistence fishing is for survival. The fish caught are eaten.

All fishing requires a license. On a charter boat, the captain's license covers the people aboard.

RYAN BEARDY

— Community Advocate / Mentor & Coordinator —

❝I use my lived experience to create a better world.❞

Ryan has overcome a lot of challenges to get where he is today. "Growing up, I didn't have goals," he says. Adverse social conditions on his reserve led him to join a gang, and he landed in juvenile detention at the age of thirteen. During his time in prison, he reconnected with traditional Indigenous healing practices and used writing as a creative outlet. He also got his high school diploma and decided gang life wasn't for him.

When he was released, Ryan applied to university and, a few years later, received his degree in political science. He began volunteering for political leaders and started some **grassroots organizations**, which led to opportunities to speak to the Senate about justice issues. He went on to write articles for the *Globe and Mail*, the Canadian Broadcasting Corporation (CBC), and *VICE Magazine*.

Ryan's lived experiences have helped him to become what he is today: an advocate for his community and a coordinator of mentors for New Paths, part of the Gang Action Interagency Network, which helps current gang members find a way out.

SPIN-OFF JOBS

★ Guidance counselors work in schools to give students the skills they need to succeed.

★ Outreach workers support community members, provide relief, and connect people to resources and programs.

> Community advocacy is about speaking up for people who can't do it themselves. Ryan supports and gives a voice to those who have difficulty communicating their views and feelings to others.

Ryan believes that helping is healing, which is why he began the Mutual Aid Society, an informal organization that provides food and assistance to those in need, and Healing Together, a men's wellness group facilitated by Elders. He wakes up every day excited to do meaningful work.

As the mentorship coordinator at New Paths, Ryan starts his workday by checking in with the mentors and getting them what they need to help their clients—from basketballs to school applications. According to Ryan, mentorship is about capacity building, not forcing someone to change, and his job is to advise and support the mentors. His role as a community advocate means he meets with government officials, politicians, lawyers, and other organizations to educate them on issues affecting vulnerable and marginalized youth. He also presents at schools and focuses on the power that comes with believing in yourself, even when society doesn't. Ryan is proof that with determination and grit, it is possible to create a new identity.

Ryan's dream is to leave a legacy for others and to create the programs he wishes had been there for him. As he says, "I want to plant the trees that will provide the shade for others, even if I'm not around to enjoy it."

INSPIRING INDIVIDUALS ★

THANDIWE ABDULLAH has been surrounded by strong Black women her whole life. It's no surprise that she wanted to make a difference too. At fifteen, Thandiwe Abdullah helped create the Black Lives Matter in Schools Program, which was adopted by the National Education Association in the United States. Thandiwe's biggest victory was successfully campaigning to end random searches in the Los Angeles Unified School District. She plans to continue her activist work by pursuing a law degree. "I want to transform the systems we live under from ones that oppress us to ones that empower us."

★ WHY NOT TRY ★

Filling a need in your community. The Mutual Aid Society began during the pandemic when people in Ryan's community were underserved. He connected resources like food, air conditioners in summer, and warm clothes in winter to the people who needed them.

PRO TIP

Turn negatives into positives! Ryan saw the value he could add as a mentor to young people who wanted to change their lives. His past became an essential part of building his future.

SIMON ADRIANE ELLIS

— Midwife —

> 66 What really gives me joy in my practice is being with people during times of transition. 99

What do you do when your best friend unexpectedly goes into labor, and you're the only one who can help? Simon helped their friend get through labor with the guidance of a midwife over the phone. Their friend was so impressed with how Simon handled the situation that they encouraged them to consider a career as a midwife. After some initial hesitation, Simon started taking prerequisite university science courses while they worked full time for the next several years. Simon was thirty when they entered midwifery school to become a certified nurse midwife.

There are different types of midwives, but certified nurse midwives (CNM) are qualified to practice in hospitals, birthing centers, or private practices. The extensive training of CNMs allows them to perform many of the same roles as doctors, including writing prescriptions, conducting exams, and ordering lab tests. After several years of taking prerequisite classes while working full time, Simon first became a registered nurse, then obtained a master of science in nursing. Their area of study was pregnancy experiences for transgender and nonbinary people. There wasn't a lot of research on that topic at the time, but when Simon graduated in 2012, more studies were starting to be published.

Simon has held different positions as a CNM, including three years providing family planning and launching a gender-affirming program. They now work for Quilted

DID YOU KNOW?

Midwives have been around for thousands of years. Many Indigenous cultures, such as the Māori people of Aotearoa New Zealand, had skilled midwives who understood how to mix and use herbal remedies to help during pregnancy and childbearing long before modern midwifery became a regulated profession in the 1900s.

FUN FACT

One way to gain experience with children is to take a babysitting course. For example, the Canadian Red Cross offers seven to eight hours of training to kids over the age of eleven. Participants learn first aid to handle emergencies like choking, allergic reactions, and broken bones. They also gain the skills necessary to provide responsible care for younger children. You can search online for a babysitting certification course in your area.

Health, a midwifery practice that wants everyone to have access to services that respect their values and needs during a time of transition. When Simon sees a client in the clinic, they might perform ultrasounds, run blood tests, or help with breastfeeding concerns. When Simon is on call, client care might include monitoring someone in the hospital, administering medication, and delivering babies. Simon says being a midwife can feel like playing a game of Whac-A-Mole—two days are never alike, and you can't predict what services clients might need.

The most gratifying part of Simon's work is supporting people and helping them make good decisions for themselves and their families. A midwife needs to balance science skills (such as using math to figure out the correct dose of medication to prescribe) with human skills (such as comforting someone when they're scared). They also should be detail-oriented, flexible, and compassionate. Simon is happy with the work they are currently doing and wants to continue to make the world a friendlier place for trans and nonbinary people and their families.

SPIN-OFF JOBS

★ **Doulas** are non-medical people trained to physically and emotionally support someone before, during, and after childbirth.

★ **Lactation consultants** advise individuals on breastfeeding.

★ **Pediatricians** are doctors who specialize in caring for the health of kids.

★ WHY NOT TRY ★

Watching a YouTube video where kids interview a midwife to learn more about the profession.

PRO TIP

Being a good friend and supporting kids who need help is excellent practice for this kind of career.

TIAGO CATARINO

— YouTube Content Creator / Former LEGO Designer —

> 66 With imagination, you can do anything. 99

Tiago has turned a love of LEGO into not just one career, but two.

When he was a kid, Tiago loved building original creations with LEGO. During college he stumbled upon AFOLs (Adult Fans of LEGO), groups of people with online forums to share their LEGO projects. Seeing friends from his group getting jobs at LEGO, he decided to apply for the company as a model designer. Unlike most applicants, he didn't have a background in product design, but he figured it was worth a shot.

LEGO looks for creative people who collaborate well with others and know how to work as a team. After Tiago submitted his portfolio of custom creations to show his skill as a builder, LEGO had him take building and personality tests to see if he would be a good fit for their company.

PRO TIP

If you love LEGO, keep practicing! You're never too old to play.

★ WHY NOT TRY ★

Starting your own YouTube channel? While Tiago has a background in multimedia design and a master's in computer animation, he encourages anyone interested in becoming a content creator to just start! Don't worry about having the right camera or equipment.

At LEGO, there are three types of designers:
- Model designers develop the kits.
- Element designers create new bricks.
- Graphic designers work on the mini-figures, printed pieces, and stickers.

Tiago says working at LEGO was as amazing as it sounds. The team of model designers would be given information about the kit they needed to design in a briefing, then worked together to bring the idea to life. Tiago started out assisting other designers on their projects,

LIVING the DREAM

In 2017, LEGO held a design competition for their LEGO Friends line. The winner was nine-year old **SIENNA** from London. She designed a garden set with a treehouse, slide, monkey bars, and rock-climbing wall. Sienna started the design on paper but used the bricks she had to create the prototype. She went to LEGO headquarters in Denmark to see her design brought to life and even got to design a mini figure of herself that was included in the set!

but he was soon ready to take charge of his own models. While some designers used software, Tiago liked to build his models by hand. A few times a year the designers held brainstorming sessions and pitched ideas for models. During his three years at LEGO, Tiago saw sixteen of the models he worked on through to completion.

When he returned to Portugal, Tiago wasn't ready to give up LEGO, so he started a YouTube channel focused on LEGO tutorials, reviews, and creations. To gain a following, Tiago uploaded videos daily. As his subscribers and views increased, he was able to monetize his channel.

Monetization means making money from a product, like a YouTube video. One way for successful creators to monetize videos is through the YouTube Partner Program. Ads are placed before and during videos. The content creator and YouTube share in the revenue generated from the ads.

In his current job as a content creator, Tiago has the flexibility to structure his day in any way he likes. He usually works eight or more hours a day building with LEGO, filming, and editing the videos.

Whether working for LEGO or for himself, Tiago has turned a childhood passion into a real-life dream job.

SPIN-OFF JOBS

★ **Toy engineers** design and create toys that are functional and enjoyable. They usually work with a team of people.

★ **Video producers** oversee the planning and creation of film projects from movies to television to YouTube videos.

★ **Video game designers** develop the concept of a game and the elements that make it come alive for the player.

VALERIA VILLALOBOS
— Cybersecurity Analyst —

"You don't solve problems just one way."

When Valeria was growing up outside of Santiago, Chile, her family had limited access to the internet. To solve the problem, she bought equipment like cables and routers and figured out how to install them herself. Her parents recognized her natural abilities with technology and encouraged her to pursue this field in university.

To complete a three-year degree in telecommunications, Valeria took a wide range of courses. She learned about programming and data science, or informatics, which is the study of how data is transformed into knowledge. She also learned how to keep information systems safe from intruders, hackers, and cyber attacks. Her course work gave her the knowledge, but it was once she started working in the field that she *really* started learning. If she ran into a problem, or had a question, she had to figure it out herself. For Valeria, overcoming these obstacles is proof that she is learning.

LIVING the DREAM

SAMVIT ARGAWAL began learning code when he was in middle school and went on to start a YouTube channel and win hackathons, contests where competitors collaborate to engineer a solution to a challenge in a short amount of time. When he was seventeen, he started CS Remastered, a computer science tutoring program, as a way to give back to his community. The volunteer instructors at CS Remastered offer free virtual classes to kids interested in learning more about coding and programming. They have also connected with organizations like Girls Who Code and HomeFront NJ, a non-profit that fights homelessness, to offer lessons.

The tech industry is constantly evolving. In order to stay current, Valeria is always studying and training. Thanks to a positive mindset and passion for her job, Valeria doesn't mind. She's intrigued by the idea of making IT, or information technology, more human and social by making it safer. We all leave a digital footprint when we are online through our search history, emails, photo sharing, and social media connections. It's important to understand the risks involved with an online presence. Valeria wants to make sure everyone feels secure as they venture into the world of technology.

Valeria's specific field of **cybersecurity** is threat hunting and threat intelligence, which means she analyzes and improves an organization's digital security systems. She uses her skills to get around firewalls and bypass current security networks to find weaknesses. If someone else has already breached the system, she identifies possible attackers, figures out how they got through, and recommends improvements. To do this, she needs to go into the code and review it for evidence.

In addition to her work as a cybersecurity consultant, Valeria is also a professor at a university in Santiago. She's able to pass on her knowledge and experience to others, including her belief that no one gets where they want to go without a few failures along the way. As Valeria says, "The fun part of the job is the challenge!"

★ WHY NOT TRY ★

Attending a STEM camp to build skills like problem-solving, teamwork, communication, and patience. STEM integrates science, technology, engineering, and math into activities like programming a bug robot, creating a stop-motion animation, or building a catapult.

SPIN-OFF JOBS

★ Information Technology (IT) managers supervise IT support staff and offer solutions to technical problems. An understanding of how to write computer programs is important to do this job well.

★ Robotics engineers design and build robots. They write, test, and monitor the computer programs that direct a robot's actions.

★ Computer programmers use languages like C++ and Python to write the code that computer applications run on.

VANESSA PAKIUM

— Electrical Engineer —

> 66 How can I make this?
> How can I find a solution for this? 99

Vanessa grew up in Mauritius, a small island off the southeast coast of Africa. Her father was an engineer and sometimes took her to job sites with him. He showed her what he was working on and often asked how she would fix a problem. This encouragement and Vanessa's own curiosity led her to a career as an electrical engineer, a job that has her asking questions and solving problems daily.

In 2011, Vanessa received a scholarship from Carleton University in Ottawa and moved to Canada to get a bachelor's degree in electrical engineering. While in her third year, she received an internship at Nav Canada, the not-for-profit corporation responsible for air traffic control in Canada, in the Information Management (IM) department. At the end of the placement, she was given a tour of the Engineering Head Office (HO) and learned about surveillance systems. Vanessa was fascinated by the equipment used to keep track of aircraft in the skies and hoped she could return to work at Nav Canada one day. Her dream came true in 2016 when she was hired as a junior radar systems engineer.

At that time, Nav Canada was launching a project to replace twelve radar systems at airports across Canada. Vanessa was actively involved in the design reviews and meetings that ensured the new radar systems met Nav Canada's requirements. In 2021, she became the senior radar engineer on this multi-year project.

LIVING the DREAM

NATHAN JAY THOMAS was only sixteen when he graduated from Florida International University with his bachelor's degree in electrical engineering. This made him one of the youngest engineers in the United States! This award-winning teen is currently pursuing a Ph.D. with interest in nanotechnology. Nathan would like to become a patent attorney who helps individuals protect the rights to their inventions.

Vanessa manages radar installations, troubleshoots problems or issues, and adapts the radar at each airport. The new equipment must also be integrated with all the other surveillance systems at the airport, and Vanessa has to ensure they work well together. Communication is critical as she works with other departments within Nav Canada and with people outside the company, like airport staff, vendors, and contractors.

Vanessa was the only woman who graduated from Carleton's electrical engineering program in her year. Although she currently works on a team of three female engineers, she says there still aren't many women pursuing careers in engineering. She believes exposing more girls to science is essential, allowing them to build things and showing them opportunities in the fields of science and engineering.

One benefit of Vanessa's job is that it indulges her love of travel. She's visited many different places for work, including multiple trips to Italy during the early phases of her current project. Vanessa also loves having the freedom and time to study a problem and find a solution for it. She learns a lot through trial and error, then adapts as needed to make an idea work. She says that since engineers need to work with many different types of people, it's important to respect the opinions of others.

There are several departments within Nav Canada and countless opportunities for Vanessa to explore in the future. She loves that she can continue learning and becoming an expert in different areas throughout her career.

SPIN-OFF JOBS

★ Electronic technologists maintain the equipment used for air navigation.

★ Hardware design engineers design and create the physical components for computers.

★ Software developers make the programs used to run computers.

★ WHY NOT TRY ★

Building a robot from a kit to learn about circuits, batteries, lights, and switches.

VILOSANAN SIVATHARMAN

— Funeral Director —

❝ This is a service...helping people in their tough time. ❞

Vilosanan was working as an engineer in Ontario when three family members died within months of each other. His family is Tamil, originally from Sri Lanka, and a Hindu funeral service includes specific rituals. Vilosanan visited fifteen to twenty funeral homes between 2010 and 2011, but he could not find a place that offered what his family required.

Chapel Ridge Funeral Home in Markham, Ontario, was looking for multicultural funeral directors when Vilosanan discovered them. The owner encouraged him to consider attending Humber College to train to become a funeral director, and Vilosanan decided to apply. He wanted to help fill the void in the funeral business for Tamil clients and families from other cultures.

Vilosanan enrolled in Humber College's two-year Class 1 Funeral Director diploma program, which would train him to do embalming. This is the practice of preserving a body after death. There is also a Class 2 Funeral Director program that does not include embalming training.

Before Vilosanan could start his program, he was required to complete forty hours of observation at a funeral home. This would

FUN FACT There are several eco-friendly alternatives available for burials. They do not involve chemicals and focus on more environmentally friendly practices such as using biodegradable materials. Green burials are often less expensive, conserve space, and have a smaller impact on the land than typical burials do. Although these practices may not meet the needs of clients who require specific traditions, it's important that the funeral industry consider the environmental impact for generations to come.

allow him to see how a funeral home operates, understand the embalming process, and learn about the role of a funeral director. Later, once his year-long course was complete, he had to spend another year interning at a funeral home before he could receive his license. In 2014, Vilosanan became the first Tamil class 1-licensed funeral director in North America.

Funeral directors do not work a nine-to-five job. Vilosanan is called at all hours of the day or night to advise people on what steps to take after someone dies. Funeral pre-planning is considered bad luck in some cultures, and there is a stigma surrounding caring for the dead, so many people don't know what to do after a death. It's Vilosanan's job to have the deceased transported to the **coroner**'s office or to the funeral home, depending on the circumstances surrounding the death. He then works with the family and loved ones to book the chapel and arrange the visitation, service, cremation, burial, and other necessary services, including shipping human remains to other countries.

Although Vilosanan has clients from many different cultures, he is in particularly high demand from the Tamil community. He speaks the language and understands the needs of a traditional service, such as having clergy, choir, and chanters present as part of the funeral rites.

Vilosanan finds his work challenging but rewarding. He often deals with individuals who are in shock and grieving, so he must be a good listener, stay calm, and demonstrate a lot of patience. It's a career that requires dedication, but Vilosanan is glad he can offer support and guidance to his clients during difficult times.

★ WHY NOT TRY ★

Approaching a funeral home to see if they have volunteer opportunities to assist with a service.

SPIN-OFF JOBS

★ Clergy are religious leaders trained to lead prayers and religious services and offer support on spiritual matters.

★ Hearse drivers operate a vehicle used to transport the deceased to a funeral home and to their final resting place.

★ Crematorium operators are responsible for doing cremation and maintenance of a crematorium..

YUE SHI
— Ballet Dancer —

66 **Dancing makes me happy, and ballet is what I love.** 99

How do you take a dream of becoming a professional ballet dancer and turn it into a reality? For Yue, it meant setting goals and working hard to achieve them.

Yue started studying ballet at Liaoning Ballet School in Hebei, China, when he was eleven. He was serious about becoming a principal ballet dancer, the highest ranking performer in a professional dance company. As part of his training, Yue had to attend many international competitions to prove his ability. When he participated in the Jackson International Ballet Competition, he drew the attention of one of the jurors, Royal Winnipeg Ballet (RWB) Artistic Director André Lewis. Yue was invited to join the RWB School Aspirant Program as an apprentice in 2015.

Yue's progress toward becoming a professional dancer involved several steps. First, he joined the RWB Corps de Ballet in 2016 and performed as part of a large group of dancers. In 2018 he was promoted to second soloist, which meant smaller groups and some solo roles. A year later, he achieved the designation of soloist. Finally, in 2021, he reached his goal and became a principal dancer with the RWB.

Professional ballet dancers require hours of practice and dedication to develop technical skills. Yue has instructional classes at 9:30 AM, where he learns about classical and contemporary ballet. Rehearsals take place Monday to Friday from 11:00 AM to 6:00 PM, with a one-hour

★ WHY NOT TRY ★

Taking a dance class in a style that interests you.

PRO TIP

Set goals and determine the steps you need to take to achieve them. Be willing to persevere even if pain or injury delays the achievement of your dreams.

lunch break. When Yue is performing in a show, his days start later with an afternoon class followed by show notes and rehearsals before the evening performance. He has weekends free when he's not performing, a week off at Christmas, and a more extended break in the summer. Even during his time off, he continues to train and take classes to stay in peak physical condition.

Yue has won many awards throughout his career, always striving to improve himself and become well known in the dance world. He prefers classical ballet, which includes famous shows like *Swan Lake and Giselle*. Yue hopes to one day play the role of Albrecht, the male lead in *Giselle*. He loves wearing detailed costumes; his favorite is the one the prince wears in the second act of *The Nutcracker*.

Yue enjoys the challenge of expressing different emotions through his facial expressions and movements. He also loves that dance has allowed him to travel and visit many different places worldwide. Yue hopes he has many years to develop and grow as a dancer.

LIVING the DREAM

CHARLOTTE NEBRES was eleven years old when she became the first Black ballerina to dance the role of Marie in the New York City Ballet's production of *The Nutcracker*. She later wrote a picture book, *Charlotte and the Nutcracker: The True Story of a Girl Who Made Ballet History*. This book, illustrated by Alea Marley, tells the story of Charlotte's experience preparing for, and performing in, this holiday classic.

SPIN-OFF JOBS

★ Choreographers design dance routines and teach others how to perform them.

★ Costume designers create outfits worn by performers.

★ Stage managers are responsible for the details of a production—such as lighting, props, and technical cues—and ensuring the shows run smoothly.

THE CAREERS BEHIND THIS BOOK

It takes a whole team of people with different skill sets to make a published book! Here are some of the people involved in *See It, Dream It, Do It.*

Colleen Nelson & Kathie MacIssac
— Authors —

Colleen and Kathie, like many authors, have other jobs besides writing. Time management and determination are two important skills that writers need.

Gail Winskill
— Publisher —

Gail makes the big decisions at Pajama Press, like choosing which books to publish and when. She collaborated with the Authors, Editor, and Illustrator on the content, art direction, and design of the book and decided how many copies to print.

Scot Ritchie
— Illustrator —

If you love drawing and creating, you might like to work as an illustrator. Scot used reference photos provided by the Authors and worked with the Publisher and Editor to get each image just right. Like authors, illustrators often work on more than one project at a time.

Erin Alladin
— Editor —

Editors need an eye for detail and strong writing skills. Erin worked with the Authors to make the text in this book consistent and fun to read. She also worked on many of the nonfiction features like the table of contents, glossary, and index. Fun fact: Erin is an author too!

Lorena González Guillén
— Designer —

Lorena worked with the Editor and Illustrator to put together the layout and all the visual elements of this book, from the shape of the text boxes to the color of the pages. She also worked with the printing company to make sure the finished book came out just right.

Quinn Baker
—Sales & Marketing Manager —

An approachable disposition is needed for sales and marketing. Quinn made sure all the right people found out about this book, like reviewers, librarians, and the buyers who decide what goes on a bookstore's shelves. His job involves making presentations, writing press releases, organizing events, and more.

Simin Dewji
—Marketing Assistant and Proofreader —

Simin uses her creative skills to promote books through marketing activities like designing ads and creating online content. She also proofread this book once it was all put together to catch any last typos or formatting mistakes.

Liza Kleinloog
— Administrator —

Staying organized is essential for Liza. She keeps track of many things, including when staff and authors need to be paid! She also pays attention to the printing company's schedule and makes sure the finished books arrive safely in the warehouse so they can be published on time.

MEET THE EMPLOYMENT EXPERTS

There is no one "right" way to find a job, but there are lots of people who can provide support and guidance. There are many kinds of experts who know what kinds of jobs are out there and what skills employers are looking for.

School Resources for Career Advice

School guidance counselors, high school advisors, and career counselors are all trained to provide you with information and suggestions on next steps after high school. They can provide you with resources to find out what job is right for you, and they can make sure you take the correct courses.

Post-Secondary Programs

Many colleges and universities offer programs that equip students to enter specific careers, so you can learn a lot about the choices available to you by reading their websites or brochures. Most of these institutions also offer virtual tours and have open houses that go in-depth about the programs they offer. Or you might find their booth at a school career fair where students can ask staff questions to learn more.

Job Fairs

Job fairs often take place in high schools or community centers. Some are also hosted online. At these events, you can visit the booths of a variety of employers, recruiters, and training programs. You might even be given a short interview on the spot!

Hands-On Skill Development

University and college are not the only route. Some high schools provide work placement programs and life-skills classes where you learn to write a resume, apply for jobs, and set goals. Programs like 4-H, Junior Achievement, and Scouts and Guides give you skills and experience that you can use when considering what you'd like to do in the future.

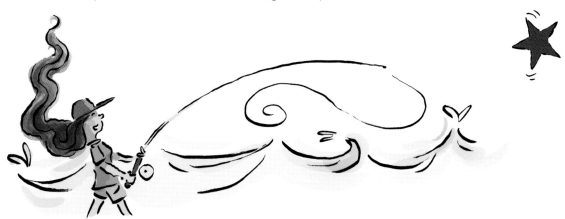

Quizzes and Assessments

There are reputable online quizzes that suggest occupations based on your skills and interests. Taking a quiz might open up possibilities you didn't know existed, or point out skills you didn't know you had. Ask a guidance counselor or advisor for some suggestions.

Professional Career Matchmakers

Some people find their dream job with the help of employment coaches or headhunters. Employment coaches will help you create a resume and network with people who are in a position to make your dream job a reality. Headhunters are people who locate and recruit individuals who meet specific job requirements. A headhunter might recognize that your talent and skills will be a good fit for a future employer.

TRY IT OUT

Even if you are years away from graduating, there are things you can do now.

Volunteer at places connected to your career interests, like summer sports camps, animal rescues, zoos, and farms.

Ask questions! If you're curious about a job, do some digging to see if it's a good fit for you. Send an email, or make a phone call, to ask your questions.

Consider your skills. What are you already good at? Having a learned skill or a natural ability will set you apart from others. It might also lead you to your dream job.

Get inspired by the young people in this book. They found a way to try out the field they love, and you can too!

Find a mentor. If you already know the job that's right for you, ask to learn from an expert.

Get your hands dirty! Learning something new like carpentry or composting might lead to a new passion, which can lead to a future career.

ACKNOWLEDGMENTS

There are always lots of people to thank when a book is published—you've met most of them in the Careers Behind This Book section. Lots of gratitude to the Pajama team, especially to Erin for her hands-on guidance, to Lorena for the masterful layout and design, and to Scot for the illustrations. A big thank you to everyone who so kindly agreed to be interviewed for this book.

Photo Credits

Page 8: Angie Aragon © Joshua Colby | Page 14: David Solano © Lerman Montoya | Page 15: Karen Weatherington © Sam Roberts | Page 16: Devapriya Chattopadhyay © Science Media Centre, IISER Pune | Page 18: Faith Fundal © Ally Gonzalo | Page 20: Hazel Barton © Hazel Barton | Page 22: Jean Nault © Kimberly Bosch | Page 28: Leigh Gardner © Tanner Hillis | Page 29: Judith Kasiama © Pavel Boiko | Page 32: Maysoon Zayid © Astrid Stawiarz | Page 33: Michael McCreary © Pete Paterson | Page 34: Melissa Haney © Donna Lynn Photography | Page 35: Isabel Fredette © Paul Fredette | Page 42: Ryan Beardy © Johnathan Ventura | Page 44: Simon Adrienne Ellis © Maxx Tomlinson | Page 54: Yue Shi © Ian McCausland

GLOSSARY

A

accessible: designed to be easily seen or used by all

apprentice: a person who is learning a trade from a skilled individual

areas of opportunity: skills that can be developed to reach goals

B

bachelor's degree: a degree awarded for (usually) four years of study at a university or academic college. Also known as a baccalaureate degree

bias: an opinion or prejudice not based on fact

C

conceptual: describing an imagined idea that can be brought to life

consultant: a person who provides expert advice

coroner: a person who investigates unusual or suspicious deaths

cybersecurity: protection against unauthorized use of electronic data

D

delegates: people who represent others

diploma: a certificate awarded to show successful completion of a course

diplomacy: the act of managing a country's interests abroad

discrimination: unjust treatment based on gender, sexuality, race, ethnicity, ability level, or culture

doctorate: the highest level of post-graduate study. People with this degree have a doctorate of philosophy (PhD) and are considered doctors

F

foreign service: a government agency that looks after a country's interests abroad. They plan, develop, and promote the country's diplomatic, commercial, and cultural policies

forensic: related to the use of science to help investigate crimes

fraud: deceitful actions that result in financial or personal gain

G

geology: the study of the physical Earth and its history

grassroots organizations: organizations started by everyday people to address an issue or make change in their community

I

internship: a short-term position that trains someone to do a job

J

job shadow: following and observing a professional in their work environment

K

kinesiology: the study of body movement

M

master's degree, or **master's**: an academic degree awarded to someone who has achieved mastery of a field of study through an additional year (or more) of study after their bachelor's degree

Métis: a distinct cultural group of mixed Indigenous and European (mainly French) heritage

night rating: certification that allows a pilot to fly at night

O

occupational therapists: health care professionals who help people find strategies to fulfill their daily routines and roles

on call: available to work when needed but not on duty

opaque: not see-through

P

philosophy: a way of thinking

post-secondary: courses or degrees taken after high school

pre-apprentice course: a program that prepares individuals for entry into apprenticeship programs

R

RCMP: Royal Canadian Mounted Police

S

surveillance: close observation of a suspect

U

undergraduate degree or **undergrad**: see bachelor's degree

underrepresented: less likely to be present, often due to societal barriers

V

vulnerable: at greater risk of harm due to social, economic, or political barriers

INDEX